2.08

Baseball: Fielding Ground Balls

By Ron Fitzgerald

D0665410

HIGH interest books

Children's Press
A Division of Grolier Publishing
New York / London / Hong Kong / Sydney
Danbury, Connecticut

For Andrew R. Smith and Frederick Exley, true fans

Book Design: Nelson Sa
Contributing Editor: Rob Kirkpatrick

Photo Credits: Cover © Angelo Barros and Nelson Sa; p. 5 © Elsa Hasch/All Sport; p. 7 © Ezra Shawn/All Sport; pp. 8, 10, 12, 13, 15 © Angelo Barros and Nelson Sa; p. 16 © Tim Shoskema/All Sport; pp. 18, 20 © Angelo Barros and Nelson Sa; p. 21 © All Sport; p. 22 © Todd Warshaw/All Sport; p. 24 © Angelo Barros and Nelson Sa; p. 25 © All Sport; p. 27 © Stephen Dunn/All Sport; p. 28 © Jonathan Daniel/All Sport; p. 34 © Al Bello/All Sport; p. 37 © Doug Pensinger/All Sport; pp. 38, 41 © Angelo Barros and Nelson Sa

Visit Children's Press on the Internet at:
http://publishing.grolier.com

Library of Congress Cataloging-in-Publication Data

Fitzgerald, Ron.
   Baseball: Fielding Ground Balls / by Ron Fitzgerald.
      p. cm. – (Sports clinic)
   Includes bibliographical references and index.
   Summary: Provides advice and instructions on choosing a glove, playing various infield positions, getting ready to catch a ground ball, and where to throw it once it is caught.
   ISBN 0-516-23360-2 (lib. bdg.) – ISBN 0-516-23560-5 (pbk.)
   1. Fielding (Baseball)—Juvenile literature. 2.Baseball—Defense—United States—Juvenile literature. [1.Fielding (Baseball) 2. Baseball—Defense.] I. Title: Ground balls. II. Title. III. Series.

GV870.F57 2000
796.357'24—dc21
                                                                00-026219

CONTENTS

INTRODUCTION

"In the beginning, I used to make one terrible play a game. Then, I got so I'd make one a week, and finally, I'd pull a real bad one maybe once a month. At the end, I was trying to keep it down to one a season."
— Lou Gehrig, Hall of Fame first baseman

When people think of baseball, many of them think of great hitters such as Mark McGwire, Ken Griffey Jr., and Sammy Sosa. Hitting is an exciting part of baseball, but it is not the only part of the game. Players also need to be able to play defense. They have to be able to field. Major leaguers such as Cal Ripken Jr., Andres Galarraga, and Rey Ordoñez help their teams win a lot of games by making great plays in the infield. To become a great infielder, you have to know how to field ground balls. It takes a lot of practice to become

Cal Ripken Jr. helps his team win games with his fielding skills.

4

comfortable fielding grounders. It also takes a lot of concentration. You have to know where to stand and how to get ready for a pitch. You have to know how to catch the ball and where to throw it. And you need to be able to do these things consistently.

Millions of kids have grown up having a baseball glove as their most prized possession. However, many of them never have learned how to use their gloves. This book will help you to turn your glove into a tool for fielding ground balls.

Shortstop Nomar Garciapara is
one of the game's exciting fielders.

ONE

TAKING THE FIELD

As you learn fielding skills, you might be tempted to try for one-handed, barehanded catches like the ones big-league stars make. But first, you need to learn the basics of fielding. You probably will make a lot of errors (mistakes that let a runner get on or advance) along the way. Keep at it. No one becomes a great fielder overnight.

The first step toward becoming a good fielder is finding a good glove.

CHOOSING A GLOVE

A lot of young players have gloves that do not fit. They often buy a glove that is too big so that they will

Baseball players can choose from
many different sizes and styles of gloves.

grow into it. However, a huge glove is hard to use. Even if you do catch the ball, it might get lost in the webbing (pocket between the thumb and index finger). You need to be able to take the ball out of the glove quickly so that you can throw it in time. Get a glove that you will be able to open and close easily.

You also want to get the right kind of glove for the position you play. Infielders usually have smaller gloves than do outfielders. First basemen have special gloves to help them catch balls at first base. Go to a sporting goods store and tell the salesperson what position you play. He or she will help you to pick out the right kind of glove.

New glove leather is stiff. You will need to break it in (make it softer) by using it before real games. You also should rub special oil for treating leather into your glove every now and then. This will keep your glove in good condition. Have the salesperson tell you how to care for your glove.

POSITIONS IN THE FIELD

The first step to fielding ground balls is knowing where to stand in the field. Each infielder has an area on the field where he or she is responsible for catching ground balls.

Shortstop and Second Base

The shortstop and second baseman are the middle infielders. They are responsible for covering the area of the field that is "up the middle" (around second base). The shortstop stands halfway between second base and third base. The second baseman stands halfway between first base and second base (see figure 1).

Figure 1: The shortstop (left) and second baseman (right) play in the middle of the infield.

11

Both middle infielders need to be quick. The shortstop has to have good hands and a strong throwing arm. If the shortstop bobbles (mishandles) a ball or throws it weakly to first, the batter might be able to beat the throw. The second baseman plays closer to first base, so he does not have to have as strong an arm. However, both players should be good at getting two outs on one play. This is called turning a double play.

Third Base

The third baseman stands a few feet to the right (from the batter's view) of third base (see figure 2). The third-base position is called the "hot corner" because third basemen have a lot of hard-hit balls go to them. The third baseman stands close to home plate—only 90 feet

Figure 2: The third-base position is sometimes called the "hot corner."

12

(27.5 m) away. Batters hit many hard ground balls to third base. The third baseman needs to be able to catch them. Then, he needs to be able to throw across the infield to the first baseman in time to catch the runner. Usually, the third baseman has the best arm of any infielder.

First Base

The first baseman stands a few feet to the left of first base (see figure 3). The first baseman does not have to be quite as good as the rest of the infield at fielding ground balls. Even if the first baseman bobbles a ground ball, he may still have enough time to pick it up, run over, and step on first base. He also can throw the ball to the pitcher, who covers first during such

Figure 3: The first baseman must field balls and catch throws at first base.

13

plays. Still, the first baseman must be good with a glove. He has to catch throws at first base from the other infielders.

The Pitcher

Many people forget that the pitcher is a part of the infield. The pitcher has to be able to field ground balls, too. This can be a very difficult job. The other infielders can prepare themselves during the pitch, but the pitcher can't. After he throws the ball, the pitcher is not in a good position to catch a ball. Also, he is the infielder closest to home plate. The ball can come back fast at the pitcher. Only pitchers with great reflexes can field ground balls.

Outfielders

Infielders are not the only players who need to catch ground balls. When the batter hits a ground ball through the infield, an outfielder must get the ball and throw it to an infielder. An outfielder must get to a ground ball quickly, though. If he sits back and waits

Figure 4: An outfielder needs to be able to get to ground balls quickly.

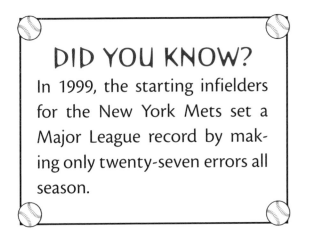
for a ground ball, a base runner can advance to the next base. An outfielder should be able to charge (run toward) a ground ball, pick it up, and then throw it—all in one fluid motion (see figure 4).

TWO

MAKING THE PLAY

You should begin preparing to catch a ground ball before the pitcher throws the ball. Then, if the batter hits a grounder to you, you will be ready to make the play.

There are three steps to fielding ground balls: get steady, get ready, and react.

GET STEADY

As the pitcher starts his windup, you need to get into a good fielding position. Bend your knees. Bend your upper body at the waist. Your legs should be apart for good balance. Keep your weight on the balls of your feet. Stay low (see figure 5). If a ground ball comes your way, you will need to be close to the ground in order to catch it.

Figure 5: Mark McGwire and other Major League players try to use correct form whenever they play in the field.

Moving with the Pitch

Experienced baseball players position themselves according to the type of pitch that the pitcher is going to throw. The catcher uses hand signals to call for the type of pitch—fastball, curveball, slider, etc.—and the location—inside (close to the batter) or outside (away from the batter). The fielders see these signals and change their positions. For example, if the pitcher is going to throw an outside fastball to a right-handed batter, the batter is more likely to hit a ball toward the right side of the infield. A smart infielder might take a step or two in that direction.

GET READY

Here comes the pitch. Stay low. Keep your knees bent. Both hands should be below your knees, with your glove open to the batter.

As the pitcher throws home, take two small steps forward (see figure 6). These two steps get your body moving. It is easier to change direction if you are moving just a little bit before the ball is hit.

Figure 6: A good fielder should get ready before every pitch.

REACT

Crack! The batter makes contact. As soon as the batter hits the ball, you have to make quick decisions. Where is the ball going? Is it coming toward you? If it isn't, can you run to where the ball is going? Can someone else field the ball more easily?

If a ground ball bounces into your area of the field, take charge. Move toward the ball. A manager might tell his or her fielders, "Play the ball—don't let the ball play you!" Stay on the balls of your feet. Move fluidly but aggressively.

GETTING IN FRONT OF THE BALL

Getting in front of the ball is the most important part of fielding grounders. If your whole body is in front of the ball, you have a better chance of fielding it (see figure 7). Your hands will not have far

Figure 7: The fielder should get in front of the ball whenever he can.

20

to go to catch the ball. Also, if you bobble the ball, it may bounce off your body and stay in front of you. Then, you still have a chance to throw to first and get the batter out.

Moving Left or Right

When the ball is hit to your left or right, you still can get in front of it if you move quickly. The key to moving sideways is the crossover step. Let's say a ball is hit to your left side. Turn your body to the left. As you turn, cross your right leg in front of your body (see figure 8). This should be your first step toward the ball. Then, make your second step with your left leg. If the ball is hit to your right side, turn your body to the right and cross over with your left leg.

Figure 8: Mike Bordick uses a crossover step to chase this ground ball.

Making the Play

Beginning players often take a step sideways with the leg that is closest to where the ball is hit. This is called sidestepping. Sidestepping is fine if the ball is hit close to you. But when the ball is farther away, you will not get to it as quickly by sidestepping. If you do get to the ball, your hands might not be ready. You are likely to make an error.

Dribblers and Bunts

Not all ground balls are hit hard. Sometimes, a batter will hit a dribbler (slow-moving ball) toward you. Sometimes, if the infielders are playing deep (way back) in the infield, the batter may try to bunt. To bunt the ball, the batter slides his top hand up the barrel (thick part) of the bat. Then he places the bat level over the plate and taps the ball.

To field dribblers and bunts, you must be quick. Charge the ball, pick it up, and make a hard throw to first. If you have taken your two small "ready" steps toward home, you are already going in the right direction. If you see the batter squaring around

Figure 9: The infielder must charge a dribbler and throw it quickly.

(getting ready to bunt), start running toward the plate. You will get to the ball sooner.

INTO THE GLOVE

As you prepare to catch a ground ball, keep your glove down in the dirt. Point the fingertips of your glove at the ground, with the glove open to the ball. Keep your glove below the ball as it bounces toward you (see figure 10). Then, as the ball takes its last bounce, bring your glove up if you need to. You never want to let a ball go underneath your glove. It is easier to bring your glove up than it is to bring down your glove.

As the ball goes into the web of your glove, close your fingers around the ball. This step keeps the ball from popping or rolling out of your glove. You also can use your throwing hand to help trap

Figure 10: Keep your glove down as the ball comes to you.

the ball in your glove (see figure 10). Then you can take the ball out of your glove quickly and throw it.

The best infielders don't stab or grab at a ground ball. They catch the ball and cushion it inward to their bodies. This is called having soft hands.

The One-Hand Catch

The surest way to catch a grounder is to use both hands. However, you can't always get both hands on the ball. If a grounder is almost out of your reach, you will have to lunge or dive with one hand outstretched (see figure 11). Also, you only use one hand when you backhand the ball.

Figure 11: Sometimes, the best way to field a grounder is with one hand.

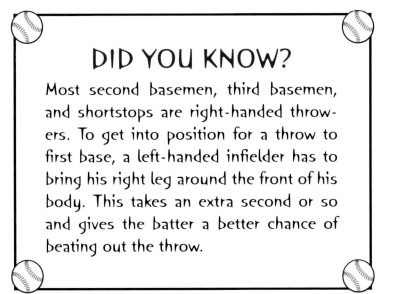

DID YOU KNOW?

Most second basemen, third basemen, and shortstops are right-handed throwers. To get into position for a throw to first base, a left-handed infielder has to bring his right leg around the front of his body. This takes an extra second or so and gives the batter a better chance of beating out the throw.

The Backhand Catch

You use a backhand catch when a ground ball is hit to the throwing-hand side of your body. Move your glove hand across your body and toward the ground at the same time. Turn your wrist so that the web of your glove is open to the ball. Again, the fingertips of your glove should point toward the ground (see figure 12). As you look down, you will see the back of your glove. Make sure to open your glove wide.

Figure 12: An infielder must be able to make backhand grabs.

THE THROW

You might make a great play catching a ground ball. But if you don't make a good throw, your play isn't worth anything. Infielders have to be good at both catching and throwing a ball.

You do not throw just with your arm. You throw with your whole body. The first part of the throw is to plant the foot that is on the same side as your throwing arm. Then you step toward the base to which you're throwing. You step with the leg on the side opposite your throwing arm. A right-handed thrower plants his right foot and steps toward the base with his left leg.

FIELDING STRATEGY AND DRILLS

If you are an infielder, you must know what is going on at all times in the game. How many outs are there? How many balls and strikes does the batter have? Who is the batter? Is he a fast runner or a slow one? Are there any runners on base? What is the score? The answers to these questions determine what you will do when the ball is hit to you. Before the pitch, you should know what to do if the ball comes to you.

A smart player will put himself or herself in the best position to make a good play. A smart manager will make sure that all of his or her players are in the correct position before the pitch.

Smart players like Cubs first baseman Mark Grace know where to play during all game situations.

PLAYING STRAIGHT AWAY

This is the normal position for the infielders. Imagine that there are lines that go directly from base to base. These lines are called the baselines. Normally, the infielders play behind the baselines, toward the back of the infield dirt (see figure 13). An infielder can run down a lot of ground balls from this spot. Meanwhile, he can get to ground balls in time to throw out the batter.

The first baseman can play a little deeper than the rest of the infielders can. He does not have to worry as much about having time to throw the ball. However, he must stay close enough to the base so that he can get there to catch throws from the other infielders.

PLAYING IN

In baseball, runners can lead off (take steps away from) the base during the pitch. A lead gives the runner a head start if the batter hits the ball. If there is a runner on third base with less than two outs, the

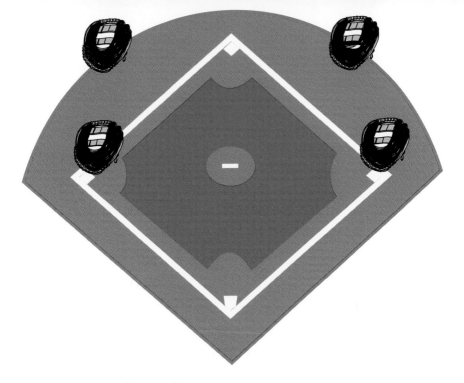

Figure 13: (above): Infielders playing at normal depth
Figure 14: (below): The infield playing in

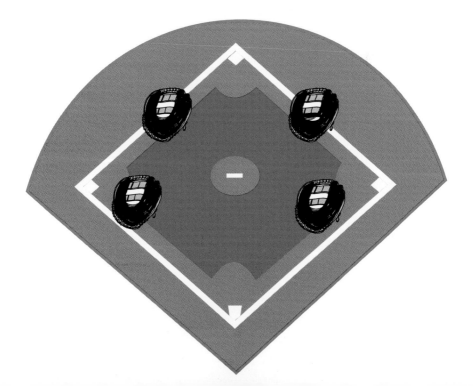

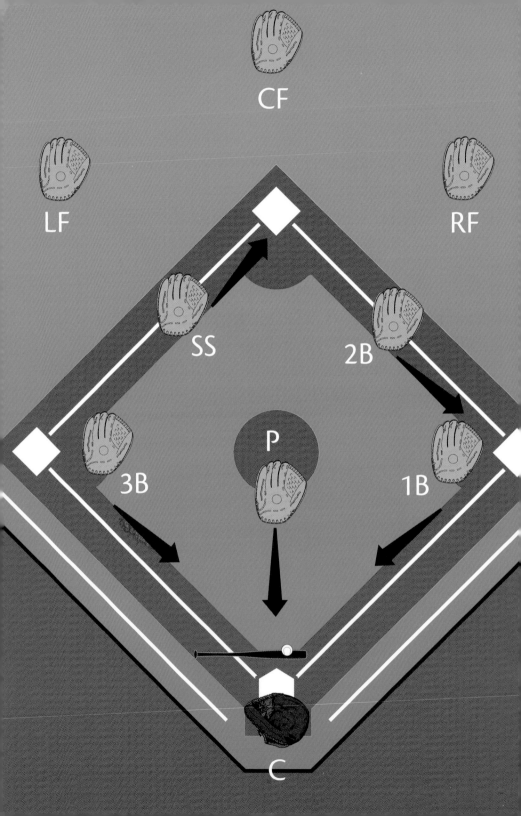

CF

LF

RF

SS

2B

P

3B

1B

C

manager might want to give his team a better chance of throwing out the runner at home. The infielders play inside the baseline, closer to the batter (see figure 14). By positioning themselves closer to home plate, they will be able to get to ground balls sooner.

The manager gambles when he plays his infield in. He gives his players more time to throw the ball when they catch it. But he also gives his players less time to react to a batted ball. If the batter hits a ground ball, it has a better chance of going into the outfield.

Infielders should only play in if there are less than two outs. If there are two outs, infielders should play straight away. They can field ground balls and throw to first base for the third out to end the inning.

Playing for the Bunt

If it looks as though the batter will bunt, the corner infielders (the third and first basemen) play way in. In fact, when they see the batter squaring around to bunt, the corner infielders run toward home plate. This puts them in the best position to field the bunt.

Figure 15: When a runner is on first and the batter goes to bunt, the corner infielders charge, the shortstop covers second, and the second baseman covers first.

When the first baseman charges toward the batter, the second baseman runs to cover first base. Then, the player who fields the bunt can throw to first base and get the out (see figure 15). If there is a runner on first base and the batter bunts, the shortstop runs to cover second. If there is a runner on second base, the third baseman stays back, and the pitcher charges the bunt.

DOUBLE-PLAY DEPTH

The double play is called the pitcher's best friend. A double play can kill a big inning for the team at bat. When the team at bat gets a runner on first base with less than two outs, a manager will put his infielders in position to turn a double play.

Up the Middle

The middle infielders should set up for a double play. The shortstop and the second baseman stand a little closer to second base. This is called "cheating" toward the base. If one of them has to field a ground ball, the

Turning a double play is one of the most important skills for a middle infielder to have.

other needs to be able to run to second base and take (catch) the throw. He steps on the base to get out the runner from first. Then he throws to first to get out the batter. If the batter hits a ground ball close to second base, a middle infielder can catch the ball, run to second base, step on the base for one out, and then throw to first for the second out.

DID YOU KNOW?

In the big leagues, the middle infielder often steps over or around second base before throwing to first on double plays. This is called a "phantom tag." Umpires usually let fielders use a phantom tag because it prevents the fielder from getting hit with the cleats if the runner slides into second base.

Figure 16: The pitcher will throw to the first baseman to hold on the runner.

Third to Second to First

When the infield sets up for a double play, the third baseman takes a few steps to his left. This makes up for the fact that the shortstop is cheating toward second base. If the third baseman gets a ground ball, he throws to second base. The second baseman takes the throw and then throws to first. This type of double play is called going around the horn.

Holding on the Runner

When a runner is on first, the first baseman will stand on (or next to) first base (see figure 16). This is called holding the runner. If the first baseman holds the runner, the pitcher can try to throw to first and get out the runner. This makes it harder for the runner to steal second base. However, it also keeps the first baseman from cheating toward second base.

FIELDING DRILLS

The best way to practice fielding ground balls is to have someone hit them to you. However, you may want to try some other drills, too. For the following drills, you need only a baseball and one or two friends:

The Quick Flick

A young infielder often takes a long time to get the ball out of his or her glove. This drill should help you to develop quick hands. Take a position in the infield. Put a friend at first base. Drop a ball on the ground in front of you. Then, pick it up and make a good throw to first as fast as you can (see figure 17). Do this several times and see how quick you can get at throwing.

Wall Ball

This drill helps you to get better at moving from side to side. Find a wall or a fence. Mark off a goal. Have a friend try to throw grounders past you and into the goal. See how many balls you can keep from getting

Figure 17: The "quick flick" drill is a good way to practice handling and throwing the ball.

through to the goal. Take ten throws and then switch. You also can do this drill in a field. Use cones or shirts to mark the goal. You may want to have more than one ball so you aren't chasing one ball again and again.

Slow Rollers

This drill will help you to field weakly-hit grounders. Form a triangle with two friends. Have a friend roll the ball slowly toward you. Charge in, field the ball and make the throw to your other friend. Take turns rolling, fielding, and catching balls.

Ground ball drills will help you to become a smooth fielder.

barrel the thick part of a bat

baselines imaginary lines connecting the bases

bobble to fumble or mishandle

break in to make a glove softer

charge run toward

cheat toward when a fielder stands closer to a base for a possible play

corner infielders the third baseman and first baseman

cover a base be on a base to catch a throw

crossover step stepping across your body; the first step you take when chasing a ground ball

double play when fielders get two outs on one play

dribbler a weakly-hit ground ball

error a mistake in the field that lets a runner get on base or move to the next base

hold the runner when the first baseman stands on (or near) first base when a runner is on first

infield in when infielders play inside the baseline

inning when each team tries to score before getting three outs

lead off when a runner take steps away from the base

middle infielders the shortstop and the second baseman

play deep when infielders play behind the baseline

straight away the normal position for infielders

webbing the pocket of a glove, between the thumb and index finger

FOR FURTHER READING

Cluck, Bob. *Play Better Baseball: Winning Techniques and Strategies for Coaches and Players.* Raleigh, NC: NTC/Contemporary Publishing, 1998.

Jordan, Godfrey P. *Kid's Book of Baseball Revised and Updated: Hitting, Fielding, and the Rules of the Game.* Secaucus, NJ: Carol Publishing Group, 1999.

McCarthy, John P., Jr. *Youth Baseball: The Guide for Coaches and Parents.* Cincinnati: Betterway Books, 1989.

Stewart, John. *The Baseball Clinic: Skills and Drills for Better Baseball—a Handbook for Players and Coaches.* Short Hills, NJ: Buford Books, 1999.

Sullivan, George. *Glovemen: Twenty-Seven of the World's Greatest.* New York: Atheneum, 1996.

RESOURCES

Organizations
Little League International Headquarters
P.O. Box 3485
Williamsport, PA 17701
(570) 326-1921
Web site: *www.littleleague.org*

PONY Baseball and Softball International Headquarters
300 Clare Drive
Washington, PA 15301
(724) 225-1060
Web site: *www.pony.org*

Web Sites
Frozen Ropes Training Center
www.frozenropes.com
This is baseball instructional school for kids of all ages.

RESOURCES

National College Athletic Association

www.ncaa.org

Find school team schedules and view stats of your favorite teams and players.

INDEX

INDEX

About The Author

Ron Fitzgerald is a freelance writer living in New York City.